Scavenger Guides

NEW YORK CITY

AN INTERACTIVE TRAVEL GUIDE FOR KIDS

Also available

Scavenger Guides Chicago
Scavenger Guides Washington, DC

Scavenger Guides

NEW YORK CITY

AN INTERACTIVE TRAVEL GUIDE FOR KIDS

Daniel Ireland

Three Leaf Press
www.threeleafpress.com

Front cover photography: New York City Skyline and Brooklyn Bridge © kuosumo - Fotolia.com.

Back cover photography: Statue of Liberty 2 © Tristinh - iStockphoto.com.

Photos courtesy of and copyright Free Range Stock, freerangestock.com: Chance Agrella 16.

Photos courtesy of Morgue File, morguefile.com: Kevin Connors 2, 3, 7, 8, 30; Carolina Jimenez-Garcia 6; Michael Connors 11, 21, 36, 62; Rose Vita 12, 71; Joe B 15; Scarab 22, 67; Ivan Melenchon 32; Karen Castens 35; Charlie Wrenn 49; Seeman 68.

Photos published under Creative Commons Attribution 2.0 Generic: Ralph Hockens 24; Susan Kane 29; Tom Thai 40; Shelley Panzarella 46; Marcin Wichary 50; Tony Hisgett 58; David Goehring 72. Photos published under Creative Commons Attribution-ShareAlike 2.0 Generic: Alan Wu 9; Ed Schipul 39; Tomas Fano 45; Daniel Bonatto 55; Kent Wang 56. Photos published under Creative Commons Attribution-NoDerivs 2.0 Generic: Tim Norvell 61.

All other photos by author unless otherwise noted.

Published by Three Leaf Press
www.threeleafpress.com

Printed in the United States of America

First edition
ISBN: 978-0-9845866-2-2

CONTENTS

SCAVENGER ADVENTURE PLEDGE

I pledge to discover the natural, historical, and cultural beauty of the places I visit, to preserve them by respecting all local rules and customs, and to share my knowledge and experiences with others.

_____

(print name here)

A NOTE TO PARENTS

Many parents have reservations about traveling with children, but travel doesn't have to end when you start a family. Travel is a wonderful time for children to learn and grow - no matter their age. It is also a wonderful time to grow as a family.

Traveling as a family is an incredible experience! Your child will grow in their knowledge and understanding of the world in which they live, and you'll see the world in a whole new way - through the uninhibited eyes of your child. Embrace traveling with your children, and you may find that your kids are capable of much more than you imagined!

This travel guide is for children visiting New York City and their parents. It is designed to engage your child in their travels and enhance their observational skills. Presented as a scavenger hunt, this interactive travel challenge will also help parents capture those teachable moments while traveling. This guide contains many interesting facts and useful pieces of information to help your child learn about New York City, but its most important role is as a tool to jump-start dialogue between you and your child.

This book is not a comprehensive travel guide to New York City. Most children would rather experience the sights and sounds of a region first-hand than read about them in the pages of a travel book. There are numerous guides available on how to get to New York City, where to stay, where to eat, and what to see and do, but they are written for adults. Use those guides to plan your trip. Cross-reference the places you plan to visit with the locations presented in this Scavenger Guide, and you will be well-prepared for a more in-depth travel experience with your child.

Each section of this guide presents several "clues" that challenge your child to find certain locations, identify items, or complete experiences throughout New York City. Each completed item earns 10 points. At the end of their travels, children add up their points and collect their award certificate. For some children, the challenge of the hunt is motivation enough. As a parent, you may wish to attach an additional reward, such as money for a souvenir or the opportunity for the child to choose where the family dines their last night of vacation. You know your child best. Be creative. Above all, have fun and enjoy this truly unique travel experience with your child!

Family travel can be both fun and informative.

Have a wonderful trip!

WHERE IS NEW YORK CITY?

New York City is located on a large harbor on the Atlantic coast of the northeastern United States. More people live in New York City than in any city in the United States.

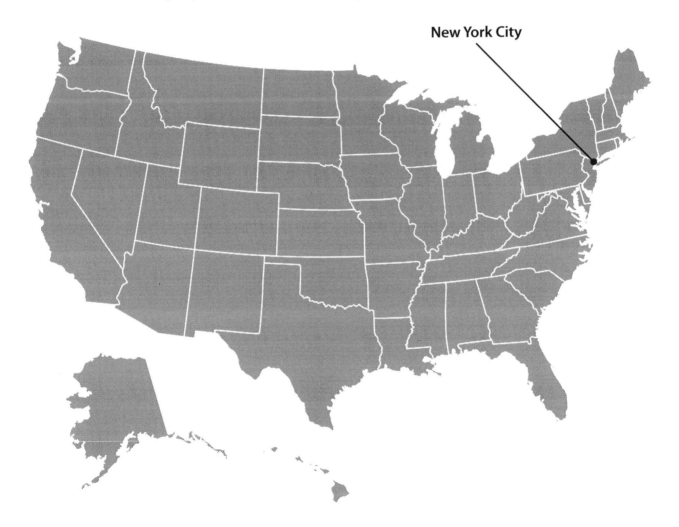

A SCAVENGER ADVENTURE

1

Start spreading the news! You're going to New York City! And there's no place better to have an adventure. This scavenger hunt will help you get the most out of your experience. Can you complete each item and become a Scavenger Guides World Explorer?

Welcome to your Scavenger Hunt Adventure around New York City! You'll need to use your eyes and your brain to solve these challenges. Your scavenger hunt will take you to many of the most popular and famous museums, landmarks, and other places of interest that make New York City such an exciting place to visit. Whether you like history, art, nature, or just experiencing new places, you'll find plenty to do in New York City.

Have fun on your hunt and good luck. You will have an absolutely wonderful time exploring this great American city!

How It Works

Your Scavenger Hunt Adventure has many challenges for you to complete during your visit to New York City. You do not have to answer the challenges in order. Feel free to skip around as you visit various locations around the city. Also, don't feel you need to complete all the challenges in one day! New York City is a big place, and it will take a lot of time and effort to complete your Scavenger Hunt Adventure. Correctly complete as many of the challenges on your scavenger hunt as you can. Keep track of each task you complete, then add up your points to win!

Before You Begin

Read all the questions in your Scavenger Hunt Adventure before you start. This will help you get familiar with all the different challenges you will be asked to complete at a specific location. This will also help you use your time more efficiently and minimize repeated visits to

▲ View of the skyline from New York Harbor.

New York City served as the capital of the United States in the 1780s before it was moved to Philadelphia and then Washington D.C.

the same site.

HELPFUL HINTS

Here are some suggestions to help you in your search:

✔ Read each scavenger hunt question carefully before you begin.

✔ Questions have been grouped by topic. Mark the questions that go with the areas you plan to visit each day. Do this each morning as you plan your day.

✔ Look carefully all around you before you record your answers. Sometimes a second search will reveal things missed at first glance.

✔ Ask the staff at a museum or site's information desk. They can often point you in the right direction.

✔ Check out a site's map for clues.

✔ Question a guard or police officer.

▲ Times Square in New York at night.

The New York subway system is the largest mass transit system in the world. It runs 24 hours a day.

✔ Read signs and plaques carefully. They often reveal clues that will lead you to the answer.

✔ Check to see if the site has a computer information system for visitors to use.

✔ Look in gift shops. The postcards and books there often cover the site's main points of interest.

✔ Don't be afraid to ask your parents and siblings for help! They might see something you have missed.

When You Finish

After you have completed as many challenges as you can, add up all the points from the challenges you solved. There is a handy worksheet at the end of the scavenger hunt to help you with this task. Compare your total score with the award chart at the bottom of the worksheet and collect your Scavenger Guides Certificate.

Can you reach the level of World Explorer? Have fun on your adventure!

WELCOME TO NEW YORK CITY

New York City is an exciting place to visit! Nicknamed "The Big Apple," the city is home to numerous world-famous destinations including the Statue of Liberty, Ellis Island, Empire State Building, Central Park, and Times Square. You can also visit many world-class museums like the Metropolitan Museum of Art and American Museum of Natural History. The city is very ethnically diverse. Residents of New York come from every country on earth with differing cultures. New York City is also home to the United Nations and is an important center for international affairs. Here are our picks for the Top 10 Things for Kids in New York City!

TOP 10 NEW YORK CITY ATTRACTIONS

#10 Rockefeller Center

Rockefeller Center was originally known as Radio City. This complex of buildings, developed during the Great Depression, is home to some of New York City's most famous landmarks including Radio City Music Hall, NBC Studios, and the seasonal ice skating rink in the sunken plaza.

#9 Fifth Avenue

The popular stretch of Fifth Avenue in the heart of Midtown Manhattan is a popular place to shop. Among the many swanky, expensive stores, you can find kid-friendly places like American Girl Place, Apple Computers, and FAO Schwarz, the world's largest toy store.

The Statue of Liberty was a symbol of welcome for all immigrants coming to America, as well as a universal symbol of freedom.

▲ Liberty Island in New York Harbor.

#8 Solomon R. Guggenheim Museum

The Solomon R. Guggenheim Museum, often referred to as "The Guggenheim," showcases world famous paintings, sculptures, and photos. The distinctive white spiral building, designed by Frank Lloyd Wright, is as popular to view as the works of art on display.

#7 Statue of Liberty

When people think of New York City, the first thing that comes to mind is often the Statue of Liberty. For the many immigrants that came from Europe to New

York, the Statue of Liberty was the first image they saw of America. The statue, a gift to the United States from the people of France, stands on Liberty Island in New York Harbor.

▲ **Ellis Island - Gateway to America.**

#6 Ellis Island

Ellis Island was the gateway for millions of immigrants to the United States as they passed on the way from their homeland to their brand new home in America. More than half of all Americans have a relative who passed through Ellis Island. Today, Ellis Island is an Immigration Museum and part of the Statue of Liberty National Monument.

#5 Times Square & Theater District

Times Square is one of the busiest intersections in New York City. Nicknamed "The Crossroads of the World," it is known for its many Broadway

Broadway plays and musicals are produced with no set run times, but instead continue to run as long as they are popular and bringing in money.

theatres, cinemas, and huge illuminated signs. Times Square is also the site of the annual ball drop on New Year's Eve.

#4 Metropolitan Museum of Art

The Metropolitan Museum of Art is located on the east side of Central Park. It is one of the premier art institutes in the world. Its two million works of art include pieces by Picasso, Van Gogh, Cezanne, and Rembrandt.

#3 Empire State Building

The Empire State Building is the tallest

▲ NYC's Empire State Building.

The Empire State Building is struck by lightning up to 100 times in a year.

skyscraper in New York City and one of the tallest in the world. It has 102 stories and stands 1,454 feet tall. Zoom to the top in elevators that travel up to 1,000 feet a minute. Then enjoy the stunning views of the city from the outdoor observatory.

#2 Central Park

In the midst of the hustle and bustle of

the city, Central Park offers residents and tourists a peaceful oasis. It is the most visited urban park in the United States. In addition to its natural setting, it is also home to the Central Park Zoo and the Metropolitan Museum of Art.

#1 American Museum of Natural History

The American Museum of Natural History opened in 1871 and today is one of New York City's most-visited family attractions. With a collection of over 32 million specimens, it's a must-see place for those

▲ **American Museum of Natural History.**

who love animals and science.

DISCOVER NEW YORK CITY

Whatever you decide to do, New York City is an exciting city to visit! Have fun, and don't forget to record your thoughts and observations in your daily journal at the back of this guide.

Ready to explore? Let's go on a New York City Scavenger Hunt Adventure!

Central Park was the first public park built in America. A competition for the park design was held in 1858.

3

CLASSIC NEW YORK

New York has been called "The City That Never Sleeps" because there is always something happening in the city. There is so much to see and do! New York City is home to many things, including tall skyscrapers, diverse ethnic neighborhoods, and world-famous parks and museums. What comes to mind when you think of New York City? For many people, visiting the city's famous landmarks, such as the Statue of Liberty, Empire State Building, and Brooklyn Bridge, is first on their list. These sites are among the top tourist destinations in the city. Others enjoy simply strolling amongst the massive skyscrapers enjoying the sites, sounds, and tastes of the city. There's always something new to discover in New York City!

BROOKLYN BRIDGE

The Brooklyn Bridge is one of the oldest suspension bridges in the United States and the first one to be made of steel.

At the time it was completed in 1883, it was the largest suspension bridge in the world. The Brooklyn Bridge links Manhattan and Brooklyn over the East River. It has become one of the iconic symbols of New York City.

1 Find the four large cables that stretch from the two towers to suspend the Brooklyn Bridge above the East River.

....10 points ☐

2 When it was first completed, the Brooklyn Bridge included two outer lanes for horse-drawn carriages, two middle lanes for cable cars, and an elevated center walkway. Take a stroll on the elevated walkway and imagine you are in the year 1883.

....10 points ☐

3 Take a picture of the New York City skyline from the elevated walkway.

....10 points ☐

Con man William McCloundy was sentenced to 2 ½ years in prison for "selling" the Brooklyn Bridge to a tourist in 1901.

▲ On the Brooklyn Bridge's elevated walkway.

EARLY NEW YORK

It's hard to imagine New York City as wilderness, but that's exactly what it was hundreds of years ago. The region was once inhabited by the Native American Lenape tribe. It wasn't until the 1620s that the Dutch West India Company, lured by the abundant beaver population, established a fur trading post called New Netherland. In 1626, Peter Minuit, Director-General of New Netherland, purchased Manhattan Island from the Lenape for $24 worth of trinkets, beads, and knives. It would later be called New Amsterdam.

New Amsterdam survived until 1664, when the English conquered the area and renamed it New York after James, Duke of York. The colony grew and prospered, surviving the American Revolution to become the first national capital of the United States.

▲ Manhattan was once a vast, unsettled wilderness.

EMPIRE STATE BUILDING

When the Empire State Building opened in 1931, it was the tallest building in the world. Today, it is still the tallest building in New York City, standing 1,250 feet tall. On a clear day, you can see for almost 80 miles from the 102nd floor observatory. Floodlights illuminate the top of the building at night in colors chosen to match seasonal events, such as green for St. Patrick's Day and red, white, and blue for the Fourth of July.

❹ Take an elevator to the 86th or 102nd floor observation decks and enjoy a 360 degree view of the city.

....10 points ▢

❺ Find a picture of King Kong, the huge gorilla from the 1933 film, climbing to the top of the Empire State Building.

....10 points ▢

❻ Find the Old Glory plaque on the 86th floor observation deck. What do the five medallions at the bottom of the plaque represent?

_____

....10 points ▢

HOT DOG VENDORS

New York is famous for its street food. If you are ever hungry, there is always a food cart nearby. From hot dogs and pretzels to carts that sell ethnic food such as Middle Eastern and Chinese, New York's street food is excellent!

❼ Find a hot dog vendor.

....10 points ▢

❽ Find a person with a cart selling ethnic food.

....10 points ▢

9 Buy lunch from a cart vendor and eat on the street like a New Yorker! What did you eat?

_____

....10 points ☐

NEW YORK BAGELS

Jewish immigrants brought bagels to New York in the 1880s. Today New York City is famous for great tasting bagels! Did you know that New York bagels are boiled in water before they are baked? They are often served with lox, a thin salmon fillet that has been cured.

10 Have your picture taken in front of a New York bagel shop.

....10 points ☐

11 Eat a New York-style bagel. Can you eat the whole thing?

....10 points ☐

STATEN ISLAND FERRY

One of the best ways to see the sites of the city is from a boat on the harbor. The Staten Island Ferry travels between Staten Island and Manhattan. During the 25 minute ride, you'll pass Governors Island and the Statue of Liberty with great views of the skyscrapers of Lower Manhattan. Get your camera ready!

12 Find an aquarium at the Staten Island Ferry Terminal.

....10 points ☐

13 Take a picture of the Statue of Liberty from the ferry.

....10 points ☐

14 Have a family member take your picture on the ferry with the New York skyline in the background.

....10 points ☐

⓯ Find the name of the ferry you are riding and write the name below:

_____

..............................10 points ⬭

STATUE OF LIBERTY

For the many immigrants that came to New York from Europe, the Statue of Liberty was the first image they saw of the United States of America. The statue was a gift from the _French government to the people of the United States in 1886 as a symbol of international friendship. The Statue of Liberty has become a symbol of freedom and democracy._

▲ One of the best views of the Statue of Liberty is from the Staten Island Ferry.

⓰ Find out what Lady Liberty is holding in her left hand.

_____

..............................10 points ⬭

⓱ Find a bronze plaque honoring poet Emma Lazarus, with text from

The Statue of Liberty shipped from France in 350 pieces. It took four months to put together.

her poem "The New Colossus."
The poem talks about the millions
of immigrants who came to the
United States. Complete the line
from the poem below:

"Give me your tired, your poor,
your huddled masses yearning to

_____ _____ "

....10 points ☐

18 Find a statue of Frenchman Frédéric

▲ **Statue of Liberty in New York Harbor.**

**The light green color of the
Statue of Liberty's copper
covering is the result of
oxidation, a chemical reaction
between metal and water.**

Bartholdi, designer of the Statue of
Liberty, on Liberty Island.

....10 points ☐

19 Find the rays on Lady Liberty's
crown. Each one measures up to 9
feet in length and weighs as much
as 150 pounds! There is one ray
for each continent on Earth. How
many rays are on Lady Liberty's
crown?

_____

....10 points ☐

TOTAL POINTS FOR THIS SECTION

*How did you do? Add up all your points
from this section and write the number on
the line below!*

_____ **points**

NOTES

4 | CENTRAL PARK HUNT

When New Yorkers want to escape the hustle and bustle of the city, they head to Central Park. Central Park is a large public park in the center of Manhattan. It's a popular place for residents and visitors to relax and enjoy nature. At certain times each week, the park is closed to vehicle traffic and the streets fill with bicyclists, rollerbladers, joggers, and strollers. More than twenty-five million people visit the park each year, making it the most visited city park in the United States.

❶ Find Grand Army Plaza at the Gateway to Central Park. The bronze statue of what famous Civil War general stands in the plaza?

_____

....10 points ☐

❷ Find Artist's Gate, one of the many entrances to Central Park. Have your picture taken by one of the many horse-drawn carriages parked outside the gate on 59th street.

....10 points ☐

3 Find the path around The Pond, one of Central Park's seven bodies of water. Take a picture as you cross the water on the arched stone Gapstow Bridge. This is one of the most picturesque scenes in the park and is always a great photo

▲ **Gapstow Bridge in Central Park.**

Central Park was declared a National Historic Landmark in 1965 and a New York City Landmark in 1974.

opportunity!

....10 points ☐

4 Did you know there are bears in Central Park? Find the home of Central Park Zoo's most famous residents, the polar bears, and write their names below.

_____

_____

....10 points ☐

5 Pet and feed an animal in the Tisch

Children's Zoo. Which animal did you feed?

_____

....10 points 〇

6 Find the statue of Balto, a heroic husky dog who journeyed across Alaska to deliver medicine that saved a community from a diptheria epidemic. Balto made his journey in the winter of what year?

▲ **A tree-lined lane in Central Park.**

_____

....10 points 〇

7 Find the statue of Hans Christian Andersen, the famous Danish fairy-tale writer who wrote *The Ugly Duckling*. His statue features him sitting and reading to what?

The original Central Park Carousel was built in 1871. It was destroyed twice by fire before being replaced by the current brick structure in 1951.

_____

....10 points 〇

8 Find the bronze statue of a group of characters from Lewis Carroll's classic story *Alice's Adventures in Wonderland*, including the White Rabbit, Mad Hatter, and the Cheshire cat. What is Alice sitting on?

_____

....10 points ☐

9 Find a man in a black and white striped shirt rowing a Venetian gondola near The Boathouse.

....10 points ☐

10 Find Bethesda Fountain in the center of Bethesda Terrace. What figure sits atop Bethesda Fountain?

_____

....10 points ☐

11 Many statues of famous writers and poets can be seen on the Literary Walk on The Mall. Find the statue on the Literary Walk of a famous person who was not a writer or poet. (hint: He sailed the ocean blue in 1492.) Who did you find?

_____

....10 points ☐

12 Find the Victorian cottage known as The Dairy. In the nineteenth century, families came to The Dairy to drink milk and enjoy snacks. What is The Dairy used for today? (hint: Go inside!)

_____

....10 points ☐

13 Find the Central Park Carousel and take a ride on one of the fifty-eight hand carved ponies. A popular Central Park attraction since it opened 1871, the carousel was once powered by a mule and horse who walked in a hidden compartment underground below the attraction.

....10 points ☐

14 Find the oldest man-made object in Central Park, the 71-foot Egyptian Obelisk. An obelisk is a tall, narrow, four-sided, tapering monument which ends in a pyramid-like shape at the top. Nicknamed Cleopatra's Needle, it was erected on the banks of the Nile River in 1500 BC for an Egyptian pharaoh.

Central Park is completely man-made. It took 15 years and over $14 million to build the park.

▲ **Central Park's historic carousel.**

....10 points ☐

15 Find a Victorian castle sitting high on top of Vista Rock. Its name means "beautiful view" in Italian. What is the name of this magical castle in Central Park?

_____

....10 points ☐

16 Stop to watch a puppet show at the Swedish Cottage Marionette

Theatre.

....10 points ▢

17 Find Strawberry Fields, a memorial to John Lennon of the band The Beatles. What single word is found at the center of the circular memorial mosaic? (hint: It's the title of one of Lennon's famous songs.)

_____

....10 points ▢

TOTAL POINTS FOR THIS SECTION

How did you do? Add up all your points from this section and write the number on the line below!

_____ **points**

NOTES

5 BUILDINGS & LANDMARKS

New York City is well-known for its many famous landmarks such as Times Square, Rockefeller Center, Radio City Music Hall, and Ellis Island. For the many immigrants that came to New York, the Statue of Liberty was the first image they saw of America, and Ellis Island was the gateway they passed through. New York City is also know for its impressive skyscrapers. The Empire State Building was built in 1931. It stood as the tallest building in the world until 1972 when Tower 1 of the World Trade Center was completed in Lower Manhattan. In 2001, the Empire State Building once again became the tallest building in New York City after the Twin Towers of the World Trade Center were destroyed in the September 11, 2001 terrorist attacks.

CHELSEA PIERS

Chelsea Piers are a series of three historic piers located on the Hudson River. The piers served as a passenger ship terminal in the early 1900s, used by the famous ocean liner Lusitania. The piers were also the destination of the Titanic before it hit an iceberg and sank on April 14, 1912. Today, Chelsea Piers is a sports and recreational complex offering a variety of athletic activities, including soccer, basketball, rock climbing, golf, batting cages, and bowling.

1 Survivors of the *Titanic* were rescued at sea and arrived at the Chelsea Piers on April 20, 1912. Find a photo of a boat docked at the Chelsea Piers

The Chelsea Piers were the departure point for Jesse Owens and the United States Olympic team as they left for the Summer Games in Berlin, Germany in 1936.

with *Titanic* survivors aboard. What was the name of the ship that rescued the *Titanic* survivors?

_____

....10 points ☐

2 Find the archway from Pier 54, the only remaining identifiable piece of the pier where the *Lusitania* was

▲ Chelsea Pier 61 where the *Titanic* was scheduled to arrive in 1912.

docked and the *Titanic* survivors were dropped off.

..............................10 points ☐

3 Find the only place you can ice skate year-round in Manhattan. What is the name of this ice rink?

_____

..............................10 points ☐

CHRYSLER BUILDING

The Chrysler Building is a skyscraper in

▲ **The Great Hall on Ellis Island.**

downtown Manhattan. It is considered by some to be the finest example of the glamorous and elegant Art Deco architecture. When it was completed in 1930, it overtook the Eiffel Tower in Paris as the world's tallest man-made structure. It is still the tallest brick building in the world.

4 Look way, way up and find the gargoyles perched on the edge of the Chrysler Building's 31st and 61st floors. The gargoyles are modeled after parts found on Chrysler automobiles, like hood

Only a small portion of Ellis Island is in New York. 80% sits within the state of New Jersey.

ornaments and radiator caps.

....10 points ☐

5 Find a plaque in the lobby honoring Walter P. Chrysler, founder of the Chrysler Automobile Corporation.

....10 points ☐

6 Find an automobile assembly line on the ceiling mural in the lobby.

....10 points ☐

Ellis Island

Ellis Island was the gateway for over twelve million immigrants coming to the United States from 1892 to 1954. Ellis Island was known as the "front door to freedom." It was here that immigrants were accepted into the United States. Today, almost half of all Americans can trace a relative that came through Ellis Island.

7 Visit the Ellis Island Immigration History Museum and find the Great Hall, where immigrants were processed.

....10 points ☐

8 Find the "Treasures from Home" exhibit, a collection of personal items immigrants brought with them to America. If you were leaving your home forever, what item would you take with you?

_____

....10 points ☐

9 Find a statue of Annie Moore, the first immigrant to pass through Ellis Island in 1892. Annie was a 15-year-old girl from Ireland who came to America with her brothers to meet their parents, who had come to New York two years earlier.

....10 points ☐

FIFTH AVENUE

Fifth Avenue runs through the heart of New York City. The section in Midtown Manhattan between 49th and 59th streets is a popular place to shop. Many high-end stores line Fifth Avenue, making it one of the most expensive streets in the world.

10 Find a building with an apple on it.

..............................10 points ▢

11 Play a song on the giant dance-on

▲ The Main Concourse inside the historic Grand Central Terminal.

Don't call it Grand Central Station! That is actually the name of the subway station beneath the terminal.

piano keyboard at FAO Schwarz, the world's largest toy store.

..............................10 points ▢

12 Find a street performer on Fifth Avenue. Have your picture taken with the performer.

..............................10 points ▢

GRAND CENTRAL TERMINAL

Grand Central Terminal is a major transportation hub for New York City. It first opened in 1913 as a railroad terminal at the time when long-distance train travel was popular in the United States. Today, it's a meeting place for train, subway, and bus traffic. Five to six million commuters pass through the terminal daily. Besides train platforms, Grand Central Terminal contains restaurants, delis, bakeries, newsstands, food markets, and retail stores.

❸ Find the famous mural of the stars on the ceiling of the Main Concourse. The 60 largest stars mark the constellations. For years they were lit with 40-watt light bulbs that had to be changed regularly by climbing above the ceiling. Today they are illuminated with fiber optics.

....10 points ☐

❹ Test out the whispering gallery located on the dining concourse near the famous Oyster Bar & Restaurant. Choose a family

member and stand in opposite corners of the large arched entryway. Now face the corner and whisper. They should be able to hear your voice as if you were right next to them!

....10 points ☐

❺ Find the room known as the "Kissing Room" where, in the 1930s and 1940s, passengers would get off the train and greet their loved ones with kisses and hugs. What is the real name of this room?

_____

....10 points ☐

GROUND ZERO

Ground Zero is the site of the former World Trade Center complex which was destroyed in the September 11, 2001 terrorist attacks. Located in Lower Manhattan, the site is currently being rebuilt and is both a memorial to the victims of the attacks and an active construction site.

16 Find Freedom Tower, a 1,776 foot tall skyscraper being built on the site of the former World Trade Center. Freedom Tower is due to be completed in 2013.

..............................10 points ☐

17 Find the large, square memorial pools marking the spot where the two World Trade Center towers once stood. The pools, called *Reflecting Absence*, are part of the National September 11 Memorial honoring the thousands of men and women who died as a result of the terrorist attacks.

..............................10 points ☐

18 Visit the 9/11 Memorial Preview Site to learn about 9/11 and the plans for the Memorial and Museum currently being built at the World Trade Center site.

..............................10 points ☐

ROCKEFELLER CENTER

Rockefeller Center was named after John D. Rockefeller, Jr., who developed the historic plaza starting in 1930. Located in Midtown Manhattan, Rockefeller Center is home to some of New York City's most famous landmarks and attractions, such as Radio City Music Hall and NBC Studios. It was declared a National Historic Landmark in 1987.

19 Find the world-famous Ice Rink at Rockefeller Center that opened Christmas Day in 1936. (hint: It's only frozen in the winter.)

..............................10 points ☐

20 Find a gold statue of the Greek god Prometheus, said to be the most photographed sculpture in all of New York City.

....10 points ☐

21 Find the statue of Atlas. What is Atlas carrying on his shoulders?

_____

....10 points ☐

22 Find a plaque at the plaza with a list of principles in which John D. Rockefeller Jr. believed. Complete

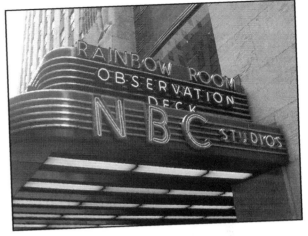

▲ **NBC Studios at Rockefeller Center.**

the principle:

"I believe that _____ is the greatest thing in the world; that it alone can overcome hate; that right can and will triumph over might."

....10 points ☐

The Top of the Rock observation platform in the GE Building is built to resemble the deck of an ocean liner.

GE BUILDING

The GE Building is the centerpiece to the world famous Rockefeller Center. It is

*the headquarters for three companies -
General Electric, RCA Corporation, and the
television network NBC.*

㉓ Find a sculpture of Zeus over the
entrance of the GE Building and
complete the message below:

" _____ and
_____ shall be
the stability of thy times."

...................................10 points ⬭

㉔ Peer into the NBC Today show's
glass-walled studios. Do you see

▲ **Fountain across from Radio
City Music Hall.**

anyone famous?

...................................10 points ⬭

**The Roosevelt Island Tramway
was featured in the 2002 film
*Spider-Man.***

㉕ Visit the Top of the Rock on
the 70th floor, a 20-foot wide
observation platform standing 850
feet above street level.

...................................10 points ⬭

RADIO CITY MUSIC HALL

Radio City Music Hall is the largest indoor theatre in the world. Millions of people have come to enjoy stage shows, movies, concerts and special events since the Music Hall opened to the public in 1932. Its nickname is the "Showplace of the Nation."

26 Find Radio City Music Hall's famous marquee - a full city-block long!

..............................10 points ⬜

27 Find the famous high-kicking Rockettes dancers in the series of six plaques on the wall under the marquee. The plaques, created by sculptor Rene Paul Chambellan in 1932, represent scenes typical of international ethnic performances of the 20th century.

..............................10 points ⬜

28 Find the 2-ton chandeliers in the lobby - considered to be the largest chandeliers in the world.

..............................10 points ⬜

ROOSEVELT ISLAND TRAMWAY

Get a birds-eye-view of the Manhattan skyline from the Roosevelt Island Tramway. Climbing 250 feet in the air, the Roosevelt Island Tramway spans the East River connecting Roosevelt Island to Manhattan. Get your camera ready! The 4-minute ride offers incredible views of New York City!

29 Take a picture of the Manhattan skyline from the Roosevelt Island Tramway.

..............................10 points ⬜

30 In 2010, the tramway was closed for six months to upgrade and modernize the system. Everything was replaced except for the towers that hold up the tram cables. How many towers are there? (hint: You can count them as you ride past on the tram!)

....10 points ☐

31 The tramway follows its route on the north side of what bridge?

....10 points ☐

St. Patrick's Cathedral

Saint Patrick's Cathedral is the largest gothic-style Catholic cathedral in the United States. The elaborate Cathedral is constructed of white marble. It is longer than a football field with tall spires rising 330 feet. If you're lucky, you can catch one of the free organ concerts offered at the Cathedral.

32 Find St. Patrick in the enormous bronze doors of the cathedral.

....10 points ☐

33 Find a window named after a flower. What is the name of this window?

....10 points ☐

34 Find a bust of Pope John Paul II commemorating his visit to the city in 1979.

....10 points ☐

35 Find the replica of Michelangelo's *Pieta* sculpture, three times the size of the original in St. Peter's Basilica in Rome.

....10 points ☐

United Nations Headquarters

The United Nations strives to bring all

nations of the world together to work for peace, justice, and the well-being of all people. Although it is in New York City, the land used by the United Nations Headquarters is considered international territory. The United Nations has its own security force, fire department, and postal administration.

36 Find a blue and white United Nations flag. What is in the center of the flag?

....10 points ☐

37 Send a postcard back home to a friend with a United Nations stamp. These stamps can only be mailed from the United Nations.

....10 points ☐

38 Find a piece of the Berlin Wall in the U.N. garden.

........................10 points ☐

▲ The central nave inside Saint Patrick's Cathedral.

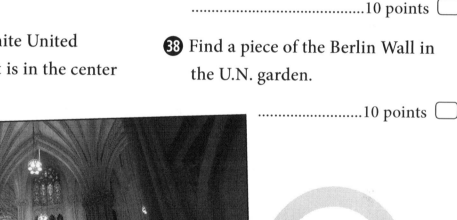

Famous funerals at St. Patrick's Cathedral have included those for Babe Ruth, Vince Lombardi, and Robert F. Kennedy.

YANKEE STADIUM

Yankee Stadium is home to the New York Yankees professional baseball team. Opened in 2009, the stadium was made from 11,000 pieces of Indiana limestone. The outside was made to look similar to the original Yankee Stadium built in 1923. Based in the borough of the Bronx, the Yankees are one of the American League's oldest franchises. Founded in Baltimore, Maryland in 1901 as the Baltimore Orioles, the team moved to New York City in 1903.

39 Find the New York Yankees historical logo, created for the team in 1947 by Henry Alonzo Keller. What type of hat is on the logo?

_____

....10 points ☐

40 Find a monument honoring Yankee great Lou Gerhig in Monument Park.

The new Yankee Stadium opened in 2009 and replaced the original stadium across the street that had been used since 1923.

▲ Catch a game at Yankee Stadium.

..............................10 points ▢

41 Find a player whose number was retired and write their name and number below:

_____

..............................10 points ▢

TOTAL POINTS FOR THIS SECTION

How did you do? Add up all your points from this section and write the number on the line below!

_____ **points**

NOTES

6 | EXPLORING THE CITY

Although New York is made up of five boroughs (Manhattan, the Bronx, Brooklyn, Queens and Staten Island), within those boroughs are individual New York neighborhoods, each one having its own distinct personality and appearance. Little Italy, in lower Manhattan, is the place to go for all things Italian! Chinatown is home to one of the highest concentrations of Chinese people in the Western hemisphere. Immigrants from China began settling in the area in the 1850s. In addition to its numerous ethnic neighborhoods, New York City is also home to other distinct areas including the financial center Wall Street, the historic South Street Seaport, and the bustling Times Square district.

CHINATOWN

The Manhattan neighborhood of Chinatown is the favored destination point for Chinese immigrants. It is home to one of the largest concentrations of Chinese people in the Western hemisphere. It is also one of New York City's oldest and most historic neighborhoods. Walk through the narrow, winding streets to explore fruit and fish markets, shops full of knickknacks and sweets, as well as hundreds of restaurants offering authentic Asian cuisine.

▲ **Shop on busy Mulberry Street in Chinatown.**

❶ Find Kim Lau Memorial Arch in Chatham Square, built to commemorate Chinese-Americans who lost their lives in World War II.

..............................10 points ☐

Going for dim sum is usually known in Cantonese as going to "drink tea."

❷ Find the huge golden Buddha in the Mahayana Buddhist Temple. Buddhism is the predominant religion in China.

..............................10 points ☐

❸ Visit a fruit and vegetable stand in Chinatown and explore the exotic

AMERICA'S MELTING POT

Millions of immigrants came to America during the late 19th and early 20th centuries seeking a better life. Most passed through Ellis Island where they were examined by doctors for disease and other potential disabilities. By 1924, over 16 million immigrants had entered the United States here. The Lower East Side, often called the "Gateway to America," was the most densely populated place in the world. You can visit the Ellis Island Immigration Museum and the New York City Tenement Museum to learn more about the lives of those that came to America.

▲ New York's Little Italy.

Today, New York remains an ethnically-diverse city. Experience multicultural New York by visiting some of its many ethnic neighborhoods such as Chinatown, Little Italy, and El Barrio.

varieties for sale.

..............................10 points ☐

4 Find a store selling chopsticks.

..............................10 points ☐

5 Eat a traditional Cantonese meal of dim sum featuring small, sample-size portions of food. What was your favorite?

_____

..............................10 points ☐

LITTLE ITALY

Generations of Italian-Americans make their home in Little Italy. Italian immigrants began coming to New York City in the late 1800s when unemployment and poverty in Italy forced many to start a new life in America. Mulberry Street is considered the heart of Little Italy. Walk the narrow streets beneath the fire escapes past turn-of-the-century tenement homes, restaurants, bakery shops, and stores. The best thing about Little Italy is the food. Try a snack of gelato, Italy's version of ice cream, or Tiramisu, an Italian cake. Yum!

6 Find St. Patrick's Old Cathedral, established in 1809.

..............................10 points ☐

7 Visit an Italian grocery and smell the aromas inside - musky cheeses hanging from the ceiling, salty Italian ham, and olives in brine.

..............................10 points ☐

8 Find Lombardi's, the first ever pizzeria in the United States (1905).

..............................10 points ☐

SOUTH STREET SEAPORT

Historic South Street Seaport is located on the site of what was once the busiest port in

America. Today, South Street Seaport mixes the past with the present. Visit the South Street Seaport Museum to get a glimpse of what early life was like in the original port of New York City. The area features some of the oldest architecture in downtown Manhattan. You can even visit historic ships at the dock including a 1893 schooner and a fully-rigged cargo ship. Then enjoy the street performers, free outdoor music, markets, and parks that make the area such a fun place to visit today.

9 Find the Titanic Memorial Lighthouse, a monument honoring the passengers and crew who died when the luxury passenger liner sank after colliding with an iceberg on April 15, 1912.

....10 points ☐

10 Find a printer at work in Bowne & Co. Stationers, a 19th-century print shop. What is he printing?

_____

....10 points ☐

11 Board a historic ship on Pier 16 and walk in the footsteps of early sailors.

....10 points ☐

12 Have an adventure in the nautical-themed Imagination Playground.

....10 points ☐

TIMES SQUARE

Times Square is one of the busiest places in New York City. Signs, lights, people, cars, buildings - it's hard to take everything in on this famous block! Times Square and the surrounding area is also the home of Broadway theatre where you can see a live play or musical on stage. Times Square is one of the most popular tourist destinations not only in New York City, but in the entire world.

13 Find the famous Madame Tussauds Wax Museum. What is holding up the Madame Tussauds sign?

......................................10 points ⬜

14 Find "The World's Greatest Toy Store" and ride the 60-foot indoor Ferris wheel, complete with flashing neon lights and themed cars inspired by favorite children's toys and characters.

The first famous ball-lowering from the One Times Square's rooftop pole was held on New Year's Eve 1907.

Which car did you ride in?

......................................10 points ⬜

15 Find a 50-foot-wide, two-story-high wall of chocolate in M&Ms World, New York City's largest candy store.

......................................10 points ⬜

16 See a show at the New Victory Theater, New York's theater for

▲ Huge signs light up Times Square.

kids and families, or the Disney-sponsored New Amsterdam Theatre. What show did you see?

....10 points ⬭

WALL STREET

Wall Street is the financial district of New York City and the financial center of the United States. It is the home of the world's largest stock exchange, the New York Stock Exchange, and the Federal Reserve gold vaults located 80 feet below street level.

Wall Street got its name from a stockade, or wall, built in 1653 by Dutch colonists to protect their settlement.

▲ **New York Stock Exchange.**

17 Have your picture taken in front of the New York Stock Exchange.

....10 points ⬭

18 Find the Federal Hall National Memorial. Federal Hall served as the first capitol building of the United States and was the site of George Washington's inauguration as the nation's first President. What famous document was signed and adopted at Federal Hall in 1789?

_____

....10 points ⬭

⓳ Find the *Trinity Root* sculpture at Trinity Church, made out of a giant sycamore that had stood for nearly a century in the churchyard before it was destroyed on September 11, 2001.

....10 points ⬭

⓴ Find the 9/11 memorial exhibit "Healing Hearts and Minds" inside St. Paul's Chapel, the oldest surviving church building in Manhattan (1766).

....10 points ⬭

TOTAL POINTS FOR THIS SECTION

How did you do? Add up all your points from this section and write the number on the line below!

_____ **points**

NOTES

7 UNCOVER NEW YORK'S MUSEUMS

*I*f you like museums, New York City is the place for you! New York City has some of the top museums in the world. Collections of the finest artwork from world-famous artists like Picasso, Van Gogh, and Rembrandt can be seen at the Metropolitan Museum of Art. If modern art is your thing, check out the Museum of Modern Art, known by the locals as the MoMA. You can board a real World War II aircraft carrier and a guided nuclear missile submarine at the Intrepid Sea, Air, and Space Museum, then spend an afternoon digging for dinosaur bones at the American Museum of Natural History.

AMERICAN MUSEUM OF NATURAL HISTORY

Across the street from Central Park stands the American Museum of Natural History, one of the largest museums in the world. Its 25 interconnected buildings cover four city blocks! Inside you'll find exhibition halls, including the kid-

favorite Dinosaur Wing, Mammal Halls, a planetarium, research labs, and a library. The museum's collection is so large (over 30 million species) that only a small fraction can be displayed at any given time.

1 Find the Star of India, the biggest blue star sapphire in the world. Where was the Star of India found?

_____

....10 points ☐

▲ **The Milstein Hall of Ocean Life in the American Museum of Natural History.**

The Rose Center for Earth and Space features a seven-story-tall glass cube that encloses the enormous Hayden Planetarium Sphere.

2 Find the 63-foot Great Canoe in the Grand Gallery. How many cedar trees were carved to create the Great Canoe?

_____

....10 points ☐

3 Find a replica of the largest animal ever to roam the earth. What is the name of this mammal? (hint: You won't find it in Mammal Halls.)

_____

....10 points ☐

BROOKLYN MUSEUM

The Brooklyn Museum is the second-largest art museum in New York City, and one of the largest in the United States. Its extensive exhibits celebrate the art of world cultures. The museum is famous for its collections of Egyptian and African art.

4 Find American painter Gilbert Stuart's portrait of George Washington.

....10 points ☐

▲ **The Brooklyn Museum is one of the largest art museums in the United States.**

5 Find the *Yoruba Beaded Crown* from Nigeria, Africa. This crown was made for a Yoruba king, or oba. What sits atop the crown?

_____

....10 points ☐

6 Find a Banta mask from Guinea. This long headdress is made to represent man's interaction with nature, combining representations of the jaw of a crocodile, the face of a human being, the horns of an

The Brooklyn Museum opened in 1897. It was originally intended to be six times its current size.

antelope, and the curved tail of a chameleon. Can you find all four of them in the mask?

....10 points ☐

INTREPID SEA, AIR, AND SPACE MUSEUM

Walk into a piece of history when you board the World War II aircraft carrier USS Intrepid at the Intrepid Sea, Air, and Space Museum. Located at Pier 86, this is New York City's largest museum. Exhibits focus on the four themes of water, space, air, and life at sea. In addition to exploring the USS Intrepid, you can crawl through the control room and attack center, dining room, and torpedo room on the USS Growler submarine. Historic aircraft are displayed on the flight and hangar decks including the famous Concorde jet that flew from New York to London in under three hours. Don't miss the Exploreum's hands-on exhibits where you can climb a cargo net, transmit messages using Morse code, and try performing various tasks while wearing space gloves. You can even experience a flight simulator and fly a supersonic jet airplane!

7 Visit the USS *Intrepid's* historic fo'c's'le, the forward-most part of the ship, and find the massive chains that hold the ship's two 30,000-pound anchors.

....10 points ☐

8 Sit inside the life-sized model of *Gemini 3* and image what it was like to travel into space in the tiny little space capsule.

....10 points ☐

9 Visit the Flight Deck and find the A-12 Blackbird with a top recorded speed of 2,269 mph. What was this plane used for?

_____

....10 points ⬭

❿ Board the "top-secret" USS *Growler* submarine and find the Crew's Mess. What did enlisted men do in this room?

_____

....10 points ⬭

▲ **Intrepid Sea, Air, and Space Museum.**

⓫ Find the Concorde Alpha Delta G-BOAD, the record-breaking plane that made the fastest Atlantic crossing by any Concorde on February 7, 1996, taking only 2 hours, 52 minutes, and 59 seconds. How fast could the Concorde fly?

_____

....10 points ⬭

The USS *Intrepid* served as a NASA recovery vessel for Mercury and Gemini astronauts in the early 1960s.

METROPOLITAN MUSEUM OF ART

The Metropolitan Museum of Art is one of the premier art institutes in the world. The museum's collection contains works from every part of the world, from prehistoric times to the present. You can view famous works of art from artists such as Pablo Picasso, Vincent Van Gogh, and Rembrandt van Rijn. The Egyptian gallery includes a whole temple that was shipped to America as a gift from Egypt in 1965.

12 Find the portrait of George Washington by Gilbert Stuart. Look familiar? The image of Washington featured in the painting has appeared on the U. S. one-dollar bill for over 100 years.

....10 points ☐

13 Find the portrait of American writer Gertrude Stein. What famous artist painted this portrait?

....10 points ☐

14 Visit the Temple of Dendur that once stood on the bank of the Nile River in Egypt about 15 B.C.

....10 points ☐

15 Find the famous painting by Emanuel Gottlieb Leutze of General George Washington's crossing of the Delaware River on December 25, 1776, during the American Revolutionary War.

....10 points ☐

16 Find Rembrandt's self-portrait. Rembrandt painted almost 100 self-portraits in his lifetime.

....10 points ☐

MUSEUM OF MODERN ART

Modern art includes artistic works from the

1860s to the 1970s. The Museum of Modern Art is considered by many to have the finest collection of modern art in the world.

17 Find the painting *Evening, Honfleur* by Georges Seurat. This work is an example of pointillism - painting with small dots of primary colors (red, green, and blue). Look closely at the sand in Seurat's painting for the many tiny dots of paint. Then back up. What color does the sand appear to be?

_____

...............................10 points ☐

18 Find *Campbell's Soup Cans* by American pop art artist Andy Warhol. How many cans of soup do you see?

_____

...............................10 points ☐

19 Find *The Starry Night*, Vincent van Gogh's painting of a quiet village before sunrise.

...............................10 points ☐

20 Find *The Persistence of Memory*, a Surrealist work of art by Salvador Dali. What is melting in the painting?

_____

...............................10 points ☐

21 Find *The Red Studio* by Henri Matisse. Look closely. Can you find

...a clock?

...............................10 points ☐

...a plant?

...............................10 points ☐

...a chair?

..............................10 points ⬭

...a plate?

..............................10 points ⬭

...a glass?

..............................10 points ⬭

...a sculpture?

..............................10 points ⬭

Solomon R. Guggenheim Museum

The Solomon R. Guggenheim Museum

▲ **Museum of Modern Art.**

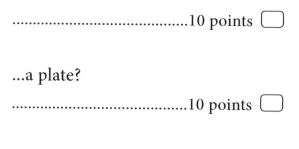

The MoMA's collection includes black & white and color photographs and approximately 22,000 films and 4 million film stills.

houses collections of world famous paintings, sculptures, and photos, but many visitors come to see the building itself. The Guggenheim Museum was the last completed project by the famous architect Frank Lloyd Wright before he died in 1959. The building is as unique as the works of art on display. Due to its unique shape, visitors walk through a part of the museum in an upward spiral, which means the artwork is always viewed from an angle.

㉒ Find *Yellow Cow* painted by German artist Franz Marc.

..............................10 points ▢

㉓ Find *Woman with Yellow Hair*. What famous artist painted it?

_____

..............................10 points ▢

㉔ Find a work of art that makes you feel happy. What is the name of the piece?

_____

..............................10 points ▢

㉕ Look up and find the skylight in the center of the museum's Great Rotunda.

..............................10 points ▢

▲ Guggenheim Museum designed by Frank Lloyd Wright.

The exterior of the Guggenheim Museum is made of gunite, a mixture of sand and cement.

TOTAL POINTS FOR THIS SECTION

How did you do? Add up all your points from this section and write the number on the line below!

_____ **points**

NOTES

8 PARKS & OUTDOORS SEARCH

New York City is a fun place to explore, but sometimes you want to escape the bustling city streets. You can at a park! The New York Botanical Gardens feature over 50 gardens to explore. If you like animals, head to the Bronx Zoo and visit the western lowland gorillas in the Congo Gorilla Forest. Historic Coney Island has roller coasters, carnival rides, and games. And just off the Coney Island boardwalk is the New York Aquarium with more than 300 marine species. There's something for everyone at New York City's parks!

BATTERY PARK

At the southern tip of Manhattan Island stands Battery Park. The park was named for the rows of cannons (artillery batteries) that were positioned there in the city's early years in order to protect the settlement.

❶ Find a circular sandstone fort that once served as America's first immigration station before Ellis

Island. What is the name of this fort?

_____

....10 points ☐

2 Find the American Merchant Mariners' Memorial. What was the memorial inspired by? (hint: Read the plaque by the sculpture.)

_____

....10 points ☐

3 Find Hope Garden, a memorial to AIDS victims.

Battery Park is one of the oldest places in New York. Dutch settlers landed there in 1623 and founded New Amsterdam.

▲ Merchant Mariners' Memorial.

....10 points ☐

4 Find *The Sphere*, a sculpture that once stood in the World Trade Center Plaza. Who is it a memorial to?

_____

....10 points ☐

Bronx Zoo

The Bronx Zoo opened its doors to the public on November 8, 1899, featuring 843 animals in 22 exhibits. Today, it is the largest urban zoo in the United States. The zoo is home to more than 4,000 animals of 650 species. The Bronx Zoo is world famous for its work in protecting endangered species.

▲ **Coney Island's classic Wonder Wheel.**

5 Find the pride of snow leopards which have been successfully bred at the Bronx Zoo. How many cubs have been born at the zoo?

The hot dog was introduced to America in 1867 when German immigrant Charles Feltman started selling them from his pie wagon at Coney Island.

....10 points ☐

6 Go on safari through the Congo Gorilla Forest, a 6.5 acre African rain forest habitat. It is home to over 400 animals including more than 20 western lowland gorillas. Using the gorilla ID plaques, write the name of your favorite gorilla.

....10 points ▢

7 Ride a giant bug on the Bug Carousel! What bug did you ride?

_____

....10 points ▢

8 Be a butterfly detective and identify three types of butterflies in the Butterfly Garden.

_____

_____

_____

....10 points ▢

CONEY ISLAND

Between 1880 and World War II, Coney Island was the largest amusement area in the United States. Millions of people visited Coney Island each year. Today, the amusement area still contains many rides and games. Three rides at Coney Island are designated New York City landmarks and listed in the National Register of Historic Places.

9 Find the Wonder Wheel, a steel Ferris wheel built in 1918. The Wonder Wheel has both stationary cars and rocking cars that slide along a track.

....10 points ▢

10 Find the world-famous Cyclone, a roller coaster built in 1927. The Cyclone is one of the nation's oldest wooden coasters still in operation.

....10 points ▢

11 Find the Parachute Jump, built for the 1939 New York World's Fair. It has been called the "Eiffel Tower of Brooklyn."

....10 points ▢

NEW YORK AQUARIUM

The New York Aquarium is the oldest aquarium in continuous operation in the United States. Opened in 1896 in Lower Manhattan, it is now located on the boardwalk in Coney Island, Brooklyn. The New York Aquarium is home to over 350 species of aquatic animals from around the world.

⓬ Find the Alien Stinger exhibit. What is one way a jellyfish uses its tentacles?

_____

....10 points ⬜

⓭ Watch an animal feeding. What animal did you see being fed, and what did it eat?

_____

_____

....10 points ⬜

⓮ Find the Aquatheater and watch a marine mammal demonstration. What was your favorite animal performer?

_____

....10 points ⬜

NEW YORK BOTANICAL GARDENS

The New York Botanical Gardens is a great place to spend the day exploring. It is considered to be one of the greatest botanical gardens in the world and is a National Historic Landmark. Founded in 1891, it features over 50 gardens, including two designed especially for kids with hands-on activities for discovering the world of plants.

⓯ Visit the Everett Children's Adventure Garden and find a plant that's shaped like an insect.

................................10 points ▢

16 Find your way through the Boulder Maze!

................................10 points ▢

17 Find the old-growth forest and take a stroll through forest which has remained untouched since before the arrival of European settlers in the 17th century.

................................10 points ▢

RIVERSIDE PARK

Riverside Park is a scenic, narrow strip

of land along the Hudson River. The park is popular with bike riders, runners, rollerbladers, and walkers. The park is a great place to view the Hudson River and New Jersey from the city.

18 Find the Soldiers' and Sailors' Memorial Monument commemorating Union Army soldiers and sailors who served in the American Civil War. It was

Be prepared to get splashed during the dolphin show. These magnificent creatures leap into the air and land with explosive force!

▲ Journey deep under the sea at the New York Aquarium on Coney Island.

dedicated on Memorial Day, 1902.

....10 points ☐

19 Find an eight-foot bronze statue of First Lady Eleanor Roosevelt.

....10 points ☐

20 Find General Grant National Memorial, better known as Grant's Tomb. Who is buried in Grant's Tomb?

_____

....10 points ☐

21 Find a life-sized statue of Saint Joan of Arc on her horse. What year was the monument dedicated?

_____

....10 points ☐

22 Riverside Park contains many gardens, playgrounds, and sports fields enjoyed by New Yorkers and tourists of all ages. Find a playground in the park and take

▲ Grant's Tomb in Riverside Park.

Ulysses S. Grant was an American Civil War general and the 18th President of the United States.

time out to play!

....10 points ▢

TOTAL POINTS FOR THIS SECTION

*How did you do? Add up all your points
from this section and write the number on
the line below!*

_____ **points**

NOTES

PARENT CLUES

Parents, here is your chance to contribute to the hunt! Use the spaces below to add additional clues for your child to solve in and around New York City. Try including places to find, foods to try, or experiences to enjoy. Have fun!

_____

_____

10 points ☐

_____

_____

10 points ☐

_____

_____

10 points ☐

_____

_____

10 points ☐

10 points ☐

10 points ☐

10 points ☐

10 points ☐

10 points ☐

10 points ☐

10 points ☐

10 points ☐

10 points ☐

10 points ☐

10 points ☐

10 points ☐

10 points ☐

10 points ☐

10 points ☐

10 points ☐

NOTES

HOW DID YOU DO?

It's time to be rewarded for all your hard work! Use the area below to add up your total points from each section. Then add up your grand total and claim your award! Fill out your name and today's date on the award certificate. Then have your mom or dad sign it. Great job!!

CLASSIC NEW YORK _____ POINTS

CENTRAL PARK HUNT _____ POINTS

BUILDINGS & LANDMARKS _____ POINTS

EXPLORING THE CITY _____ POINTS

UNCOVER NEW YORK'S MUSEUMS _____ POINTS

PARKS & OUTDOORS SEARCH _____ POINTS

_____ **TOTAL POINTS**

550-849 POINTS .... TRAVEL GUIDE
850-1099 POINTS .... TRAVEL ADVENTURER
1100+ POINTS .... WORLD EXPLORER

CERTIFICATE OF TRAVEL EXCELLENCE

This award certifies that

_____

has successfully achieved the level of

TRAVEL GUIDE

in Scavenger Guides New York City Scavenger Adventure

_____   _____
DATE   PARENT

TRAVEL GUIDE
550-849 POINTS

CERTIFICATE OF TRAVEL EXCELLENCE

This award certifies that

_____

has successfully achieved the level of

TRAVEL ADVENTURER

in Scavenger Guides New York City Scavenger Adventure

_____   _____
DATE   PARENT

TRAVEL ADVENTURER
850-1099 POINTS

Certificate of Travel Excellence

This award certifies that

_____

has successfully achieved the level of

WORLD EXPLORER

in Scavenger Guides New York City Scavenger Adventure

_____   _____

DATE   PARENT

**WORLD EXPLORER
1100+ POINTS**

KEEPING A TRAVEL JOURNAL

Keeping a journal of your travel adventures is a wonderful way to preserve memories. It makes a great souvenir of your trip to New York City! The following section of this guide provides you with space to record your daily writings.

Make a habit to write in your travel journal each night before bed. As you record your thoughts, reflect back on your day. Use your five senses to describe your adventures! What did you see? What smells filled your nose? Are there sounds that caught your attention? What tastes did you experience? What touches and textures do you remember?

If possible, take pictures each day during your travels. Photographs from your trip will complement your journal. If you do not have a camera of your own, ask your parents if you can be involved taking pictures with them.

When you return home, be sure to check out the free digital story tutorials on the Scavenger Guides website. You will learn how to combine recordings of your daily journal writings with digital pictures from your trip to create a multimedia travel video starring you! Visit http://www.scavengerguides.com to learn how!

The following page shows a sample journal entry. This is only an example. Feel free to record anything you wish from your travel experiences. Have fun with your journal!

MY TRAVEL JOURNAL

DATE _June 22_

SIGHTS _skyscrapers, lots of people, neon signs, Times Square_

SMELLS _flowers, fresh bagels, pizza!!_

SOUNDS _cars honking, people talking_

TASTES _salty popcorn, sweet candy_

TOUCHES _cold water, soft grass_

DAILY LOG

Today we walked through Times Square. There were a lot of people there and a lot of flashing neon signs and billboards too! We went to a Broadway show. It was a lot of fun. After it was done, my dad took me into the M&M Store and bought me candy! Yum!! We also walked through Central Park. We ate popcorn and played in a playground. Central Park was so peaceful. It was my favorite part of the day!

MY TRAVEL JOURNAL

DAY 1

DATE _____

SIGHTS _____

SMELLS _____

SOUNDS _____

TASTES _____

TOUCHES _____

DAILY LOG

_____

_____

_____

_____

_____

_____

MY TRAVEL JOURNAL   DAY 2

DATE _____

SIGHTS_____

SMELLS_____

SOUNDS_____

TASTES_____

TOUCHES_____

DAILY LOG

_____

_____

_____

_____

_____

_____

MY TRAVEL JOURNAL

DAY 3

DATE _____

SIGHTS_____

SMELLS_____

SOUNDS_____

TASTES_____

TOUCHES_____

DAILY LOG

_____

_____

_____

_____

_____

_____

My Travel Journal   Day 4

Date _____

Sights_____

Smells_____

Sounds_____

Tastes_____

Touches_____

Daily Log

_____

_____

_____

_____

_____

_____

MY TRAVEL JOURNAL

DATE _____

SIGHTS_____

SMELLS_____

SOUNDS_____

TASTES_____

TOUCHES_____

DAILY LOG

_____

_____

_____

_____

_____

_____

MY TRAVEL JOURNAL   DAY 6

DATE _____

SIGHTS_____

SMELLS_____

SOUNDS_____

TASTES_____

TOUCHES_____

DAILY LOG

_____

_____

_____

_____

_____

_____

MY TRAVEL JOURNAL   DAY 7

DATE _____

SIGHTS_____

SMELLS_____

SOUNDS_____

TASTES_____

TOUCHES_____

DAILY LOG

_____

_____

_____

_____

_____

_____

MY TRAVEL JOURNAL

DAY 8

DATE _____

SIGHTS_____

SMELLS_____

SOUNDS_____

TASTES_____

TOUCHES_____

DAILY LOG

_____

_____

_____

_____

_____

_____

MY TRAVEL JOURNAL   DAY 9

DATE _____

SIGHTS_____

SMELLS_____

SOUNDS_____

TASTES_____

TOUCHES_____

DAILY LOG

_____

_____

_____

_____

_____

MY TRAVEL JOURNAL

DATE _____

SIGHTS_____

SMELLS_____

SOUNDS_____

TASTES_____

TOUCHES_____

DAILY LOG

_____

_____

_____

_____

_____

_____

MY TRAVEL JOURNAL   DAY 11

DATE _____

SIGHTS_____

SMELLS_____

SOUNDS_____

TASTES_____

TOUCHES_____

DAILY LOG

_____

_____

_____

_____

_____

_____

MY TRAVEL JOURNAL   DAY 12

DATE _____

SIGHTS_____

SMELLS_____

SOUNDS_____

TASTES_____

TOUCHES_____

DAILY LOG

_____

_____

_____

_____

_____

_____

MY TRAVEL JOURNAL   DAY 13

DATE _____

SIGHTS_____

SMELLS_____

SOUNDS_____

TASTES_____

TOUCHES_____

DAILY LOG

_____

_____

_____

_____

_____

_____

MY TRAVEL JOURNAL   DAY 14

DATE _____

SIGHTS_____

SMELLS_____

SOUNDS_____

TASTES_____

TOUCHES_____

DAILY LOG

_____

_____

_____

_____

_____

_____

MY TOP 10

Earlier we gave you our picks for the Top 10 Things for Kids in New York City. Now it's your turn! Think about all the things you did in New York City. What were your favorites? Use the space below to record your picks for the best things to do in New York City. Complete this page the last day of your visit. You can share this list with your friends when they plan their own New York City adventure!

#10 _____

_____

#9 _____

_____

#8 _____

_____

#7 _____

_____

#6 _____

_____

#5 _____

_____

#4 _____

_____

#3 _____

_____

#2 _____

_____

#1 _____

_____

TIPS FOR TAKING GREAT VACATION PHOTOS

In addition to keeping a daily journal, you may also wish to take pictures during your travels. While your journal is a written record of your travel experiences, images are snapshots in time - visual memories to enjoy and share with others long after your vacation is over. Photographs from your trip will complement your journal and help you relive those great vacation memories!

This chapter will give you tips on how to take great vacation photos. Practice these techniques and soon you'll be taking shots like the pros. Above all, experiment and have fun with your photography!

Fun Creative Projects

After you return from your vacation you'll want to share your photos with family and friends. Pictures make wonderful souvenirs, and they are a great way to share your vacation experiences with others. There are also many things that you can do with your photos. Here are some fun activities you might consider.

✔ Create a framed collage of your favorite vacation photos to hang in your room.

✔ Design a vacation scrapbook.

✔ Create an online gallery to display your trip photos.

✔ Make your own vacation souvenir. Many online photo stores allow you to upload your digital pictures and place them on shirts, mugs, mouse pads, and other items.

✔ Combine your digital pictures and journal writings with motion effects and music to create a multimedia travel video to share with family and friends. Visit http://www.scavengerguides.com to learn how!

DON'T HAVE A CAMERA?

If you do not have a camera of your own, ask your parents if you can be involved taking pictures with them. Have your parents show you how to operate the camera. Ask if you can take some practice photos at home with their assistance. Another option is to use a disposable or single-use camera. These cameras come pre-loaded with a fixed number of photos (usually 24 or 36). When all of the pictures are taken, the entire camera is returned for processing. Single-use cameras are widely available for less than $10.

A MESSAGE FOR PARENTS

If possible, give your child their own camera to use. If that's not feasible, let them share the picture taking responsibilities with you. Spend some time before your trip showing them how to operate your camera correctly and responsibly. Have your child read the tips in this chapter, but don't over-supervise. Allow them the freedom to compose and take their own photos. You may be surprised at the pictures they take. Not only will you have a visual history of your trip from your child's perspective, but you may also find yourself in a few more vacation photos! While they certainly will enjoy the pictures you take, the experience and memories will mean more if they are fully involved in the process.

TIP #1: KNOW HOW TO USE YOUR CAMERA & SETTINGS

It's important that you know how to operate your camera before you go on your vacation. A lot of problems can be avoided if you know how your camera and all its settings work before you leave home. Here is a checklist of things to review.

▲ Take time before your trip to learn all the settings and features on your camera.

✔ Read the instructions that came with your camera, or ask your mom and dad to show you how their camera works. Know what settings to use for various shots.

✔ If your camera has a telephoto lens, find out how to zoom in and out.

✔ Learn how your flash works.

✔ Find out if there are any special features such as autofocus or red-eye reduction that can help you take better pictures.

✔ Practice using your camera by taking some pictures at home before your trip. This will help you get comfortable with your camera and learn what you can do with it.

✔ Practice keeping the camera still while taking pictures to prevent blurry photos. Breathe in while holding your camera close to your face and press the shutter button gently, so the camera doesn't shake.

TIP #2: CARRY YOUR CAMERA WITH YOU ALL THE TIME

Make it a habit to always carry your camera with you wherever you go. You never know when an opportunity for a great shot will occur. Be ready! You don't want to miss that once-in-a-lifetime moment.

✔ Take your camera along wherever you go.

✔ Carry your camera in a case with a clip or belt loops to attach to your waist. You can also use a waist or "fanny" pack. These free your hands but keep your camera within easy reach when needed.

▲ **Use the zoom feature on your camera to get in close for amazing shots!**

✔ Charge your camera battery each night or have extra batteries available so your camera always has sufficient power.

✔ Carry extra memory cards. You don't want to miss out on a great shot because your memory card is full.

▲ Try to include people in your photos along with landmarks. Here children enjoy the spray from a geyser in Yellowstone National Park.

TIP #3: TAKE LOTS OF PICTURES

One advantage of digital cameras is that you can take lots and lots of photos, and then choose the ones you like best and want to keep. Digital memory cards can hold hundreds of photos compared to the 24 or 36 shots on a traditional roll of film. Photos can be viewed almost instantly on the camera's display screen, allowing you to view pictures you've taken and delete the ones you don't like. This frees up space on the memory card for even more pictures!

✔ Take as many pictures as you can. Try different angles, zoom in, zoom out - experiment!

✔ Balance the types of photos you take. Try to take just as

many pictures of people as you do things and places.

✔ Use the camera's display screen to review the photos you just took. If you are not happy with the results, take additional pictures.

✔ Each night, review the photos you took that day. Delete ones you don't like to free up additional space on the memory card.

Tip #4: Get In The Picture

The photographer is often absent from vacation photos because they are behind the camera taking all the pictures! Use these tips to make sure you get into some of the family vacation photos.

▲ Check your camera's display screen after you take a shot. If you aren't happy with the picture, take another one.

✔ Pass the camera to someone else. Share the photography duties with other family members, such as a brother or sister. Take turns so everyone has a chance to be in some of the photos.

✔ Use your camera's self-timer to get into the photo yourself. Steady your camera on a solid object such as a table or rock, or use a tripod. Hit the self-timer and run around to get in front of the lens. Most self-timers will give you 10 to 15 seconds to get ready before the picture is taken.

✔ Use more than one camera. If several members of your family carry a camera, everyone is sure to get into some of the photos.

▲ Capture candid moments from your trip when people are unaware you are taking their picture.

TIP #5: TAKE CANDID SHOTS

Often vacation photographs look too posed with people standing in front of landmarks. Try capturing moments when people are not aware you are taking pictures. You'll get more relaxed, realistic photos that better depict your vacation experiences.

✔ Don't pose too many pictures. Rather than asking people to stop, turn, and smile for the camera, take candid pictures of them enjoying the moment.

✔ Try taking some silly photos. Catch people being goofy, but don't have them pose for the camera.

✔ When shooting landmarks, choose your point of interest and compose your photo in the viewfinder. Then catch your family "being themselves" in the foreground.

✔ Look for quiet moments to capture - mom and dad studying a map, your brother reading in the hotel, or your sister enjoying an ice cream at the park.

✔ Remember to have fun taking your vacation pictures. Don't over-think your photos - just shoot!

▲ Place your subject off-center to create a more natural balance in your photos.

Tip #6: Compose Your Shots

When you get ready to take a picture, take time to look through the viewfinder or LCD display. Take a close look to see what you are including and excluding in the photo. This is called composing the shot.

✔ Pick a point of interest, the visual focal point that is the main subject of your photo. This might be a person, such as a family member, or a thing, such as a statue or a mountain.

✔ Don't always place your subject in the center of the shot. Try shooting them off-center to the right or left for a more interesting perspective. This is sometimes called the "Rule of Thirds" because the best place to position the subject is along the outer third of the photo.

✔ Fill the rest of the frame with background which highlights where you are - a busy city street, a quiet mountain stream, or a colorful market.

▲ **Zoom in close to fill the frame and capture people's facial expressions.**

TIP #7: GET IN CLOSE

You'll get better photos if you zoom in close to your subjects. If you stand back too far, people and objects will look like tiny specks in the distance. Zooming in will allow you to capture details such as people's facial expressions. Fill the frame with only those things you want in the photo. Don't be afraid to use your feet to move closer to your subject or to get a shot from a different angle.

✔ Move in close or zoom in. Don't stand too far away. If possible, you should be within 6 feet of your subject.

✔ Back up to include more scenery. If you are including people in the picture, ask them to back up with you. Keeping them close will add depth to your photo.

✔ Include only as much of the background as is needed. Compose your shot. Is there something in the sky or the foreground you want to include?

✔ Take several photos of the same scene. Try different angles, perspectives, and settings.

TIP #8: CHANGE YOUR PERSPECTIVE

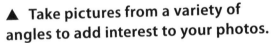

▲ **Take pictures from a variety of angles to add interest to your photos.**

Many amateur photographers take all their pictures from the same straight-on perspective. Try changing the angle from which you take a picture. Lay on the ground and shoot looking up at your subject, or stand on a chair to get a higher perspective. Don't take all horizontal pictures. Turn your camera to compose vertical shots.

✔ Experiment with different angles by looking through the viewfinder or LCD display before you take the picture.

✔ Move around. Crouch down, or stand on an object to get a picture looking down from above. Use your feet to look for creative shots!

✔ Don't back up to take pictures of tall subjects. Turn your camera to shoot vertically.

✔ Get down low and shoot vertically to compose very tall subjects (like a skyscraper).

✔ Try new things. Have fun while taking your photos!

▲ **Turn your camera vertically to take pictures of tall subjects.**

TIP #9: BE AWARE OF BACKGROUNDS

When you compose your photos, be sure to study the entire frame, not just the subject you are shooting. Make sure there is nothing distracting in the background like a lamp post or tree limb that appears to be sticking out of someone's head.

✔ Before you press the shutter button, take a moment to look at the background in the viewfinder. Does it complement your subject or is it distracting? Remember that all parts of the frame add up to make a photo.

✔ Zoom in or use your feet to move closer to your subject or use a different angle until the background is uncluttered.

✔ Use background to take interesting shots, such as a family member attempting to "hold up" a leaning building.

Tip #10: Check Your Lighting

Proper lighting can be the difference between a great shot and a poor one. Make sure you have enough light available, or use a flash. Many cameras have an automatic flash which goes on only when needed. But use your flash sparingly. Natural sunlight is best.

▲ Make sure there is nothing distracting in the photo's background, like an errant tree limb or lamp post.

✔ Keep the sun behind you or to the side. If the sun is behind your subject, it will cast a dark shadow over them.

✔ If you can't move so the sun is behind you, use your camera's flash to light your subject and minimize shadows.

✔ Keep taking pictures even if the sky turns gloomy or it starts to rain or snow. You can capture some dramatic shots during these less-than-ideal conditions.

✔ Try to avoid using a flash if possible. The flash on your camera will only light the area immediately in front of you, often resulting in poor pictures. Try shooting in low light without a flash. Use low lighting to be creative!

▲ **Shooting in low light without a flash can often yield dramatic results.**

TELLING A STORY WITH YOUR PHOTOS

Your pictures tell a story - the story of your vacation! Like all good stories, your vacation has a beginning, a middle, and an end. Make sure you cover all three in your photos. Rather than just taking a bunch of random pictures, think about how you want to "tell the story" of your vacation to your family and friends when you return home.

THE BEGINNING: START TAKING PHOTOS AT HOME

The beginning of your story includes all the planning and preparation as well as the travel to get to your destination.

Start taking pictures right away! Here are some ideas of things to shoot.

- ✔ Take pictures of family members packing bags for the trip.

- ✔ Capture your dad loading the car with luggage.

- ✔ Take a group photo of your family before you leave. Use your camera's self-timer or ask a friend to take the photo so you can be included.

▲ **Start taking pictures at the beginning of your trip - when you're packing the car, boarding the train, or waiting at the airport.**

- ✔ Get pictures of your family at the airport, boarding the train, taking the shuttle, or waiting for the bus to arrive.

- ✔ Shoot a close-up of your plane tickets or boarding passes.

- ✔ Photograph people who are part of your journey such as cab drivers, pilots, bus drivers, train conductors, and hotel staff. Catch them in action checking your bags, taking your tickets, etc.

THE MIDDLE: YOUR DESTINATION

Congratulations! You've reached your destination, as well as the middle of your story. This is the point where most people start taking pictures, but you're already deep into your photo journey. Keep documenting your travels with photos.

▲ **Shots from behind can show emotion, such as this photo at the Flight 93 National Memorial in Pennsylvania.**

✔ Take pictures of the places and landmarks you visit. Don't forget to include family members and others in some of your photos. Posed photos in front of landmarks are fine, but be sure to take some candid shots capturing people's expressions and their interactions at the location.

✔ Don't be afraid to shoot behind your subjects, capturing them looking up in awe at a snow-capped mountain or dancing to the rhythm of a street musician.

✔ Include photos along the way - in the car, on the road, at rest stops, etc.

✔ Take pictures of your hotel room, around the pool, and

at restaurants you visit.

✔ Use signs to introduce places. These serve as great
chapter titles when creating a photo
album or digital story. Take pictures
of "Welcome to..." or "You are now
entering..." signs. Photograph building
marquees, historical plaques, street
signs, and billboards. Have a family
member hold a sign in front of a
landmark.

▲ **Use signs to introduce new places
and help tell your story.**

THE END: HEADING HOME

Like any good story, your photo journey
needs an ending. Keep taking photos all the
way to the end of your vacation. Record not
only sights, but also people's actions and emotions as your
trip comes to an end.

✔ Take photos of family members repacking and loading
the car for the return trip home.

✔ Snap some final photos around your room. Capture
your family leaving the hotel.

✔ Photograph the boat, plane, train, or bus you are traveling in.

✔ Take pictures of your family at the boarding gate or collecting luggage at the baggage carousel.

✔ Capture people's emotions. Catch them napping or playing games to pass time.

✔ Take photos at rest stops and restaurants on the way home.

✔ Capture a few final shots after arriving back home. Take pictures of people unpacking the car, greeting friends and neighbors, or reuniting with family pets.

▲ **Keep taking pictures at stops on the way home. Your vacation isn't finished yet!**

HAVE FUN WITH PHOTOGRAPHY

Above all, remember that these tips are suggestions, not rules you must follow. Don't worry if you cannot remember all these tips. You can always go back and review them occasionally to refresh your memory. Experiment and have fun with your photography!

WHAT'S NEXT?

Congratulations on completing your scavenger hunt around New York City! You have uncovered clues, gathered points along the journey, and collected a well-deserved award. You have also kept a daily journal to record your travel memories and taken photos to document your adventure. Above all, you had a great time visiting New York City!

When you return home, be sure to check out the free digital story tutorials on the Scavenger Guides website. These tutorials will teach you how to record your daily journal writings and combine them with digital pictures from your trip to create a multimedia travel video. This video is sure to become a treasured remembrance of your vacation for the entire family!

If you enjoyed this scavenger hunt around New York City, check out our guides to other destinations. Visit http://www.scavengerguides.com to learn more.

Happy traveling!

▲ Gap of Dunloe, County Kerry, Ireland.

ABOUT THE AUTHOR

For as long as he can remember, Daniel Ireland has loved to travel. As a young boy, he traveled extensively throughout North America and Europe with his parents and three siblings. He now shares his passion for travel and adventure with his own family. When he's not on the road, he can be found in Grand Haven, Michigan, where he lives with his wife, Nancy, and their two children, Megan and Andrew.

10637452R0

Made in the USA
Lexington, KY
09 August 2011